BRITAIN

IN OLD PHOTOGRAPHS

BALSALL HEATH
& HIGHGATE

PAST & PRESENT

ALAN HEMMING & VAL HART
FOR BALSALL HEATH LOCAL HISTORY SOCIETY

SUTTON PUBLISHING

Sutton Publishing Limited
Phoenix Mill · Thrupp · Stroud
Gloucestershire · GL5 2BU

First published 2003

Title page photograph: Flo's Café, 1930s.

British Library Cataloguing in Publication Data
A catalogue record for this book is available from the
British Library.

ISBN 0-7509-2917-0

Typeset in 10.5/13.5 Photina.
Typesetting and origination by
Sutton Publishing Limited.
Printed and bound in England by
J.H. Haynes & Co. Ltd, Sparkford.

Mr Homer's house and tannery, Balsall Heath. Watercolour by S. Wright, 1799.

Opposite: A postcard view of Moseley Road, early 1900s.

CONTENTS

Introduction   5

1. Schools   7

2. Places of Work   17

3. Streets & Housing   29

4. Transport   41

5. Places of Worship   51

6. Leisure   63

7. Public Houses   79

8. Shops & Shopping   91

9. Events & Celebrations   109

10. The Second World War & Regeneration   119

    Balsall Heath Local History Society   127

    Acknowledgements   128

BALSALL HEATH LOCAL BOARD.

RE QUESTION OF

ANNEXATION

TO

CITY OF BIRMINGHAM.

To the Ratepayers & Property Owners

The Boundaries Sub-Committee of the City Council having proposed terms for the inclusion or absorption within the City area of the District of the Balsall Heath Local Board of Health, the Local Board have decided, before giving an answer to such proposal, to take instructions from the rate-payers and property owners of the district, at a meeting to be specially called for the purpose.

I therefore invite your attendance at such meeting, to be held at the

BOARD SCHOOLS, TINDAL STREET,

BALSALL HEATH,

On Monday Next, the 10th November, inst.,

AT EIGHT P.M.,

for the purpose of passing or rejecting the undermentioned resolution.

J. R. O. TAUNTON,

Chairman of the Local Board.

A poster advertising a meeting of ratepayers to decide on the proposed annexation of Balsall Heath by the city of Birmingham, 1891. Until 1891 Balsall Heath was a separate district from Birmingham. Parliament passed a Local Government Act in 1858 which allowed parish authorities to apply for powers to levy rates for the improvement of streets and for sanitary measures. At first the proposal was made that King's Norton parish should apply. However, there was obviously disparity of needs within the parish since it included the fast-growing district of Balsall Heath. The solution was the long-overdue separation and the first meeting of the Local Board of Health took place in October 1862, after meetings of residents and elections.

The first proposal for annexation came from Birmingham as early as 1867 but was vigorously opposed, as were later proposals in 1884 and 1887. However, it was finally agreed in 1891, when about one-tenth of the residents voted, and so Balsall Heath became a part of Birmingham.

INTRODUCTION

Open fields, a sparkling stream, blackberries, magnificent oak trees and scattered farms. This was the picture of rural Balsall Heath and Highgate in the early eighteenth century, when Moseley Road was no more than a muddy track, heavily used, however, by a procession of laden packhorses wending their way to the hungry Birmingham markets. The town was a mere smoky blot on the distant landscape and no one envisaged its remarkable growth, least of all the wealthy manufacturers who moved out of town to establish rural homes for their families away from the hubbub of their workshops. The turnpiking of Moseley Road in 1767 made the journey to town easier, and by the turn of the century Balsall Heath was clearly identifiable as 'a genteel neighbourhood' and Highgate air was said to be worth 'a guinea an ounce'. However, all was on the brink of change. Hints of future development could be heard across the fields as Birmingham pursued its ever-increasing noisy metal trades. The town had become a magnet of opportunity for all and people poured in from the countryside in search of fame and fortune.

From the 1830s the pace of change quickened as increasing demand for housing for Birmingham's growing population tempted landowners to sell up and make a quick profit. In the parts of Highgate that were nearest the town, workshops and industry began to creep outwards. Camp Hill station, at the junction of Moseley Road and Highgate Road, opened in 1840 on the new railway line from Birmingham to Gloucester and suddenly Balsall Heath was part of a much bigger world. The area became not just a country retreat but positively fashionable and 'exceedingly eligible for villa residences'. Estate agents raved over the charming surroundings, the fresh air, the woods, the picturesque countryside . . . and the rates, which were significantly lower than in the town of Birmingham.

At this time Balsall Heath was just a remote corner of King's Norton parish, but an increasingly expensive and unwelcome corner for the more rural inhabitants of King's Norton itself. By 1862 there were 10 miles of streets in Balsall Heath and a population of about 10,000. The parish officials were relieved when the Balsall Heath Local Board of Health was established. The area effectively achieved independent status from 1862 to 1891. The Board decided everything, from rubbish collection to road names, sewage disposal to street lamps.

By the 1890s, however, the writing was on the wall, as the Board entered into more and more complicated arrangements over gas and electricity supplies, piped water, sewage disposal, hospitals, the workhouse and a cemetery. Finally in 1891

Balsall Heath was annexed by the city of Birmingham after a vote by residents. In return the City promised to embellish Moseley Road with a stately new library and baths which still grace the area today.

Balsall Heath's pride in its own identity survived this ruthless annexation, however. By about 1900 just about all the open land had gone and much of the later development of housing was closely packed terraces and side avenues. It was a close-knit community bound together by ties of kinship and neighbourliness.

As for the present, Balsall Heath and Highgate today present a fascinating blend of continuity and change. Some of the fine buildings from the past still serve the area. Some, such as the library, the baths and Tindal School, still retain their original use. Some of the churches are still in their original buildings, for example St Alban's, and Edward Road Baptist Church. Some of the old factories are still using old premises and the parks are still parks.

Much, however, has changed. The area suffered badly from bomb damage in the Second World War and there was extensive redevelopment under urban renewal schemes. Great improvements have been made with refurbished and new housing and new green open spaces. Many fine new buildings have been erected too, reflecting the religious beliefs of many of the present inhabitants; for example the Central mosque, the Clifton Road mosque and the Sikh Gurdwara on Moseley Road. There are also new schools, new health centres and new community buildings such as Calthorpe Park Playcentre, St Paul's Venture, Nursery and Sure Start Centre. There are new church buildings too, including the Church Centre in Edward Road and the Highgate Baptist Church Centre.

Even more heartening is the creative adaptation of some of our older buildings for new purposes. For example the old Sames' Piano Factory building and site has been redesigned to provide a mosque, school, training centre and day nursery.

The most striking features of Balsall Heath and Highgate today are their resilience, dynamism and community spirit. Thanks to the efforts of residents, Balsall Heath Forum, local voluntary organisations and statutory agencies working together, the area has been transformed and is an amazing example of regeneration. Balsall Heath and Highgate today have much to be proud of, both past and present.

Val Hart

1

Schools

Dennis Road School (now Anderton Park School), outdoor drill exercises, 1896.

Clifton Road Junior and Infant Schools, together with new offices for King's Norton School Board, opened in 1878. The Junior School moved to new premises in 2001 and the original building is being refurbished and converted for community use.

The new Clifton Junior School on St Paul's Road, opened in 2001.

The former Clifton Infant School, Hertford Street. St Paul's Community Foundation School took over the buildings in 1973.

Clifton Infant and Nursery School, Brunswick Road, opened in 1972.

Mary Street School, which opened in 1878, was the first Board school to be built in Balsall Heath. It was renamed Belgrave School in the 1960s. The school closed in 1970, the buildings were demolished and the site redeveloped with new housing.

Heath Mount School, built across Knutsford Street, replaced Belgrave School in Mary Street and opened in November 1970. The head was Godfrey Mundy.

Tindal Street Junior and Infant School opened in 1880 to accommodate 813 children who paid fees ranging between 1*d* and 3*d*. Originally the Boys, Girls and Infants were all treated as separate schools, each with their own headteacher like other Board Schools. Tindal Schools were, however, regarded as a shining example of excellence and consistently achieved higher grants under the 'payment by results' system which lasted till 1900. The Inspector's Report of 1881 commented on the 'handsome and commodious, but unusually costly premises' and added 'the scholars are drawn from a better social class. . . . The teachers aim at mental culture rather than mere mechanical training.' Tindal School buildings were later enlarged and are still in use today.

Children at Tindal Infant School in 1939.

St Alban's Church of England Infant School, 1913. The day school originally opened in 1866.

The modern St Alban's C. of E. School, Angelina Street/Stanhope Street, built in 1962.

Joseph Chamberlain Sixth Form College opened in 1983, housed in the buildings formerly used by Mount Pleasant School.

Percy Shurmer School, Longmore Street, built in 1962–3 and named after Percy Shurmer, City Councillor and MP for Sparkbrook, who lived locally in Belgrave Road. This school now also accommodates The Play House, a Theatre in Education project. Inset: 'Our Percy, Champion of local people.'

The School of Art, Moseley Road, designed by W.H. Bidlake. This elegant building was opened in 1900 for secondary pupils of exceptional artistic talent. Despite vehement protest it closed as a school in 1975, and is currently used by the British Association of Muslims.

Stratford House was originally a farmhouse built in 1601 by Ambrose Rotton, and is still an outstanding feature of Moseley Road today. For a period from 1854 it was used as a private girls' school. The picture shows the 'South Aspect and school rooms'.

Chandos School in Highgate.

Children at Jakeman Nursery School, 2000.

Nelson Mandela School, Colville Road. It was named in honour of the African leader Nelson Mandela while he was still imprisoned in South Africa.

The prize-winning Heath Mount School netball team, early 1980s.

2

Places of Work

This magnificent brass clock was
Samuel Heath & Sons' contribution to
the Great Exhibition in 1853.

Samuel Heath & Sons' brassfounding factory in Leopold Street, established in 1830, and still flourishing today. It has been run by five successive generations of the same family and still occupies the original site.

The old design room at J.H. Butcher & Co., Moseley Road, showing the lithographic stones used in the printing of transfers. The firm originally came to Balsall Heath in 1909 and today has a worldwide reputation.

Ryland's paint and varnish factory in Haden Street, dating from 1860 and still there today.

Left: A varnish maker at Ryland's, 1911. The firm had its origins in the late eighteenth century but owed its success to the mastery of a lacquer which could be applied without heat, produced by a secret process, said to have been acquired in China.

A group of Ryland's workers, *c.* 1914.

'The Mozart Works' – Sames' Piano Factory in Woodfield Road. The firm was founded in 1855 in central Birmingham but in 1889 expanded to cheaper building land in Woodfield Road, constructing a vast three-storey factory. Sparks from the nearby railway caused fires in 1913 and 1923, the latter destroying both the roof and the business.

Above left: The old factory building and site in Ombersley Road, now used by the Hazrat Sultan Bahu Trust (UK) for education and training. A splendid mosque is also part of the complex. *Above right:* A typical Sames piano.

The Ephraim Phillips factory in Bissell Street, with uniformed delivery drivers. The firm originally started here in 1880.

The Ephraim Phillips factory today.

The former Highgate Road tram depot, which opened in 1913. At the time of the photograph in the 1980s it had been converted to a maintenance depot for ambulances.

A group of workers at Moseley Road tram depot, which opened in 1907.

The former fire station, Moseley Road, Highgate Square, which originally opened in 1912.

Moseley Road Fire Brigade, 1924.

The new Moseley Road fire station, built in 1972.

Established in 1869, the police station in Edward Road is still in operation today, together with 'blue lamp'.

Bradbury's factory in Highgate Square, originally the garden of a house fronting Moseley Road. This family firm was founded in 1859.

Elcock & Sons Ltd, metal spinners and pressworkers in Tindal Street. Another family firm, Elcock's was founded in the 1890s in a back garden workshop.

A funeral procession of Ambler's carriages. The firm was established in Longmore Street in the 1890s and moved to King's Heath in 1967.

N. Wheatley & Sons, funeral services, a long-established family firm which originally started in Station Street. It has been based here on Moseley Road for over 50 years.

The premises of Dares Brewery Limited in Belgrave Road, 1962.

Women workers at Leng's brush factory in Sherbourne Road during the First World War.

Moseley Road, showing the earlier site of Robinson's store and Malcolm House, 1924.

Robinson's Removals & Furniture Depository and Malcolm House, Moseley Road.

3

Streets & Housing

This eighteenth-century watercolour of Ball's House, Edgbaston Lane, was painted by Warren Blackham.

Darwin Street, with a typical 'court' shown on the left. This was the entrance to a number of back-to-back houses built around a courtyard, with communal water supply and sanitary arrangements. Such courts were typical of much of the earlier housing in Birmingham and were built as cheaply as possible to house the huge and rapid increase in population. Highgate had many such courts whereas development in Balsall Heath tended towards terraces, often with a further back terrace behind them or side avenues of terraces.

The entry to Court 15, Bissell Street, 1959.

Vaughton Street, with a handcart and barrow outside a greengrocer's that is typical of the local area.

St Martin's flats, Vaughton Street/Emily Street, 1942. Constructed between 1936 and 1939, the flats were demolished in 1980–1.

Longbridge Road from the corner of Sherbourne Road, 1968.

Haden Street with corner shop.

The rear of Sherbourne Road, 1963.

Chandos Road, Highgate, with Moseley Road School in the background, 1953.

Houses in Highgate Square, Moseley Road, *c.* 1905.

Houses opposite Highgate Park on Moseley Road, 2000.

A charming group of Lenches' Trust Almshouses, Conybere Street, erected in 1880. In the background can be seen St Alban's Church and Birmingham Central Mosque (left). The photograph was taken in the year 2000.

Rowton House, Alcester Street, was built in 1903 as a working men's hotel with a 6*d* a day charge. Converted in the 1990s to the attractive Chamberlain Hotel, it has now been renamed the Paragon Hotel.

Houses in Mary Street, next to the Coach & Horses public house, 2000.

Houses in Mary Street with balconies, between Strensham Road and Edgbaston Road, 2000.

Mary Street in 1970, immediately before demolition.

Modern housing in Mary Street, 2000.

Houses in Balsall Heath Road, 1964. They have now been demolished.

The leafy front gardens of houses in Balsall Heath Road, now demolished, but seen here in 1972.

A typical terrace development: Hagley Villas off
Taunton Road, dating from the 1890s. This part of
Balsall Heath was one of the last areas to be developed.
It was part of the estate of John Gregory Watkins who
died at his home, Woodfield House, Ombersley, near
Worcester, in 1890. The pattern of housing around
Roshven Road was a densely packed maze of side
avenues which ensured a good return on the
investment. However, the houses here are also noted
for their attractive decorative features.

The rear of houses in Wenman Street, 1964.

New housing in Brighton Road, 2000.

New housing in Clifton Road, 1990s. This photograph shows the symbolic handing over of the key to old housing stock that had been restored to high modern standards under urban renewal schemes.

4

Transport

A postcard view of Moseley Road showing an open-top electric tram on the route into the city. The New Inn public house is on the left.

Horse-drawn buses in Taunton Road, *c.* 1906. The first route for a horse-drawn omnibus to run through Balsall Heath to Moseley came in 1846. These were eventually supplanted by horse-drawn trams which began to appear from the 1870s. These, too, gave way to the steam trams which first arrived locally in 1885.

Horse-drawn open-top buses on the John Bright Street–Balsall Heath route in Station Street, *c.* 1893.

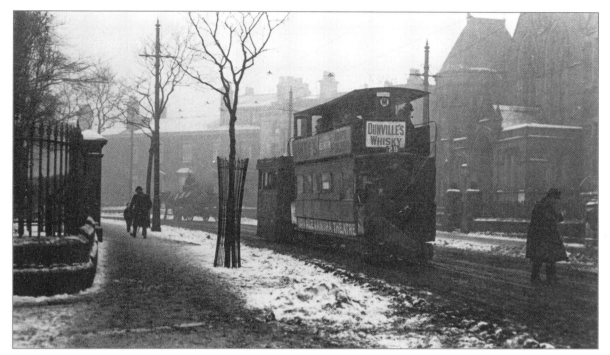

A steam tram passing Highgate Park on Moseley Road on a wintry day, 1906.

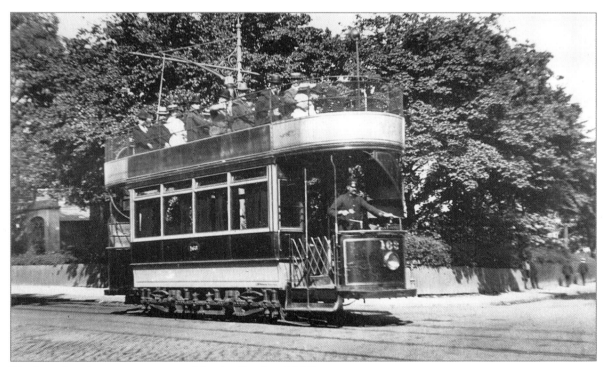

The first electric tram to serve on Moseley Road, *c.* 1907.

The Moseley Road–Trafalgar Road tram depot. It was built in 1906 to a design specially suited to this 'select and residential area'. A second depot opened in Highgate Road in 1913.

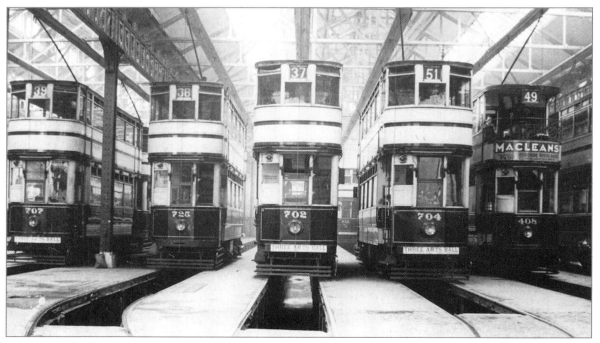

A line-up of trams at the Moseley Road depot, showing the route numbers serving Balsall Heath and Highgate, 1940s.

Trams into and out of the city on Moseley Road, 1949. Part of the Moseley Road depot is on the left.

A modern 'City 50' bus by the now disused Moseley Road depot, 2000.

Brighton Road railway station, opened in 1875 on the old Birmingham to Gloucester line. It was damaged by bombing in the Second World War and closed.

The Moseley Road entrance to Camp Hill station with Highgate House in the background, c. 1880. Behind the station and stretching to Camp Hill were extensive goods yards. The railway line is still in use but the passenger station closed after the Second World War.

Construction of the new railway bridge and the widening of Brighton Road, 1924.

Work has been completed and all is spick and span, Brighton Road.

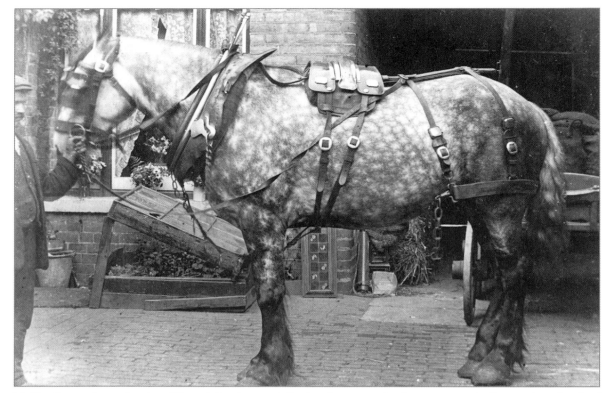

Mullis, the coal merchant in Edward Road, served the local community from purpose-built premises that had double-door entry to the yard and stables behind the family home. This picture shows his horse, *c.* 1930.

Hovis special cycle carrier by Hovis body builders, Moseley Road, *c.* 1935.

Hawley's Bakeries, Moseley Road. This large horse-drawn van was also built by Hovis, *c.* 1930.

Philip Fowler, aged thirteen, delivering milk, May Day 1930.

Mr Baker of Baker's Builders, Woodfield Road, with his builder's handcart, a common form of transport for a number of local tradesmen in the 1930s and 1940s.

Moss Bros: Moss' Meadow Dairies' handcart was built by C.H. Wedgbury of Belgrave Road.

Ephraim Phillips' delivery trucks, supplied by Balsall Heath Motor Works, Mary Street.

Traffic on Belgrave Middleway, 2002.

5

Places of Worship

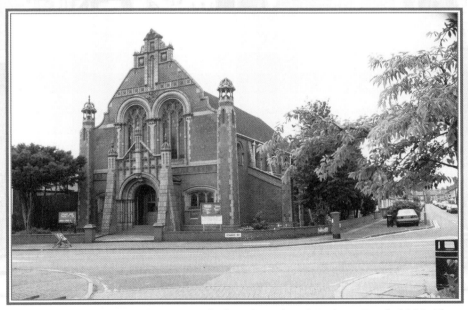

The Baptist Church on the corner of Edward Road and Harbury Road, 1900. The Baptist Chapel on the corner of Edward Road and Harbury Road was built at a cost of more than £6,000. It was erected by the congregation which had been meeting in Balsall Heath Road since 1873 and provided seating for 550 people. This photo was taken in 2000.

Moseley Road Methodist Church, on the corner of Lime Grove, 1872. This church was an off-shoot of the Cherry Street chapel in Birmingham, founded in 1782 by John Wesley. The church buildings were destroyed during bombing in 1940.

The rebuilt church as it is today.

The foundation stone for the rebuilt Methodist Church was laid in 1949 by Mrs Minnie Moon, one of the original church members who was aged ninety-one.

The Assembly of the First Born Church, in Studley Street, off Ladypool Road, 2002.

St Paul's Church, Moseley Road, on the corner of St Paul's Road, was once the popular and fashionable focus for Balsall Heath and Moseley. It opened in 1853 with seating for over 1,000, and was extended in 1856. Church schools were also established in 1856 in Vincent Street, and in Ladypool Road in 1862. In 1980 the church moved to shared accommodation at the Church Centre in Edward Road. The Moseley Road buildings were demolished and the site is now occupied by a small factory unit.

The parish magazine started in 1854 and reflected the variety of local activities – Sunday schools, Bible classes, sports, clubs, outings, charitable and missionary work.

The purpose-built Church Centre in Edward Road, on the corner of Mary Street, opened in 1980. It houses two different churches, St Paul's Church and the Church of Christ, as well as providing a day centre for the elderly together with some sheltered accommodation.

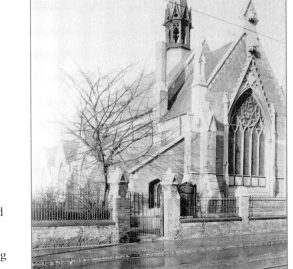

St Thomas-in-the-Moors Church, Lincoln Street, opened in 1883 with money and on land both donated by William Sands-Cox in memory of his father Edward Townsend Cox. Sadly the church was demolished during the regeneration of the area.

St Barnabas' Church, Ladypool Road, was originally a tin hut mission of St Paul's in 1890. The new building opened in 1904 but was partly destroyed by bombing during the Second World War.

St Barnabas' Church, 2002. The surviving part of the original church has been imaginatively adapted. The space at the front where the tower once stood now provides a forecourt and a vicarage.

St Alban's Church, Conybere Street, began as a small mission established in 1865 by the Pollock brothers, who were Anglican priests.

The brothers were attacked in 1867 for their high-church rituals, but stayed for twenty-five years serving the heavily populated district and were known for their remarkable pastoral work. The splendid new building was opened in 1881 and remains a landmark today visible for miles.

The old St Alban's Church.

The Society of Friends' Hall and Institute, Moseley Road, constructed at the expense of Richard Cadbury and opened in 1899. The Society of Friends had established adult classes in the area from 1876 which by 1896 were attracting an attendance of an average 810 people on a Sunday. This grand new building contained 37 classrooms, a small hall for 400, and a large hall for 2,000. It opened in 1899 when this photograph was taken.

The church at the rear of the Friends' Hall and Institute, 1899, now used by the New Testament Church of God.

Right: The Church of Christ on Moseley Road, now the Islamic Relief Centre. This originally opened in 1912 with seating for 400. It was built to replace the Chapel in Charles Henry Street which dated from 1857. In 1980 the congregation moved again, this time to the splendid new Church Centre in Mary Street, shared with St Paul's Church.

The Roman Catholic Church of St John and St Martin in George Street, established in 1896. It was originally founded from St Anne's in Alcester Street and was run by them until 1903 when it became a separate mission.

The Congregational Church of Sparkbrook, Ladypool Road, opened in 1894 as the Congregational Mission Church. The front part of the building is now a shop.

The modern Baptist Church in Highgate, seen in 2000.

The Guru Gobind Singh Gurdwara in Mary Street. This was the first Sikh temple in Balsall Heath, and was opened in 1958.

The Guru Nanak Gurdwara Bhat Singh Sabha and Community Centre, on Moseley Road, 2002.

The new mosque and associated buildings of the Khoja Shia Ithnaasheri Muslim Community, in Clifton Road. The old Congregational Church Sunday school building in Runcorn Road has been sensitively refurbished and extended as part of this development. This photograph was taken in 2002.

6

Leisure

Programme from the Moseley and
Balsall Heath Institute for 1888–9.

The new Balsall Heath Park, on the corner of Ladypool Road and Taunton Road, 1894.

Balsall Heath Park, furnished with modern play equipment, 2000.

Highgate Park, showing Rowton House in
the background, 1932.

Highgate Park, formerly Highgate Fields,
which in 1875 was the first open space
bought by Birmingham. Within a year
the 4-acre park was opened by the mayor,
Joseph Chamberlain.

The Pershore Road/Speedwell Road entrance to Calthorpe Park, complete with cannon. The park was originally parkland donated by Lord Calthorpe in 1857. This postcard view dates from *c.* 1920.

The same entrance to the park, 2000.

The Olympia, Ladypool Road, originally
known as the Ladypool Picture House. In the
early days a 'picture house orchestra' played
every evening. The name Olympia dates
from 1916 when it closed for improvements
and redecoration. In 1929–30 the cinema
was improved once more and renamed the
New Olympia, and showed the new talking
pictures. The word 'Talkies' can still be seen
on the front of the building in these photos,
taken in 1990. The cinema is now a shop.

Please Patronise Advertisers.

OLYMPIA PICTURE THEATRE,
Ladypool Road.

General Manager : - - Mr. FRANCIS E FORRESTER

Continuous Performance.

Every Evening from 6-30. Saturdays 6 o'clock

Matinees : Monday & Wednesday at 3.

Good, Clean, Moral Pictures only.
The Latest and Best.

Prices of Admission :-

Matinees, 2½, 4d. & 6. Evenings, 4d., 5d. & 7d.,

Telephone: Victoria 124. including Amusement Tax

The Hall is now thoroughly Heated and Ventilated

The Balsall Heath Picture House, later the Luxor Cinema, near Longmore Street. The advertisement dates from 1916 when films were silent but accompanied by live music. This cinema opened originally in 1913 and was one of the most expensive with prices of admission ranging from 4d to 1s. It seated 650 and in 1916 provided a full programme comprising a main feature and four short films.

A local businessman, Mr Baker, is shown seated fourth from the left in the Luxor orchestra.

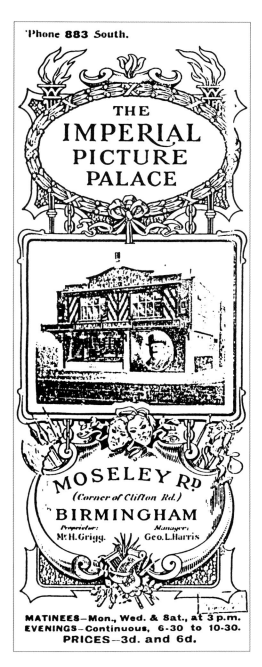

George Harris, manager of the Imperial Cinema when it opened in 1915.

The Imperial, Moseley Road, was built by Harry Grigg, a local pork butcher. From the beginning it was a huge success, and was noted for its 'select and high class audience'. The first manager was George Harris, who brought with him Mr W. Burtenshaw from Blackpool, believed to be the finest picture house pianist in the United Kingdom.

The Carlton Cinema in Taunton Road was a late arrival in the district, opening on Whit Monday, 28 May 1928. It was exceedingly luxurious, with a passenger lift to the balcony seats and a cinema organ. On 25 October 1940 it was bombed, with loss of life. The cinema reopened in December 1943, closed in 1983 and was demolished in December 1985.

The Triangle Cinema, on the corner of Conybere Street and Gooch Street, was originally known as Pringle's Palace as it was owned by Ralph Pringle, a pioneer of the cinema trade. This view shows the Triangle in 1957.

The Alhambra, Moseley Road, Highgate. This very luxurious cinema opened on 26 December 1928 with *The Scarlet Pimpernel*. It was named the Alhambra because it was built in the style of the palace of the Moorish kings in Granada, Spain. It closed on 31 August 1968.

An outing of the ABC monitors from the Alhambra Cinema, 1950s.

Vaughton's Hole on the River Rea, apparently the ideal spot for a rural dip. This was near the point where the River Rea crossed the old Kings Norton parish boundary, near the present Gooch Street. In 1745 a silver pocket watch was taken from a gentleman's clothing while he was bathing here and it was still a popular place for a swim as late as 1877. There were some drownings here in the nineteenth century. Close by was a flourishing brickyard.

BALSALL HEATH  **BATHS, PROPRIETOR,**

JOHN SMITH,

Who begs most respectfully to call the attention of the Gentry and Public in general to his newly erected Bathing Establishment; the Proprietor having studied the comfort and convenience of persons bathing has spared no expense in fitting up the Baths in the best of style; they are supplied with a continual flow of soft Spring Water; are delightfully situated in George street, Balsall Heath, a most commanding and, at the same time, a retired position, about twenty minutes walk from the centre of the Town.

Tickets for the Season, 10s. 6d.   Private Bath, 1s.   Single Bath, 6d.

Also to be Sold valuable Freehold Land adjoining the Baths, in lots of 11 or 22 yards frontage, apply as above, or at the Globe, Great Barr-street.

An illustration from *Wrighton's Directory* of 1847 advertising the private swimming baths in George Street which opened in the 1840s, and comprised a large pool and private baths.

Moseley Road Baths were built on land acquired in 1894 and opened thirteen years later in 1907. They contained a 'First Class Swimming Bath with gallery for spectators, a Second Class Swimming Bath, suites of First and Second Class Private Baths for Men and Women, a clubroom and a small Establishment Laundry'. This has been a much appreciated amenity for many years.

The interior of the first-class swimming bath.

The library, adjoining the baths on Moseley Road, opened its doors in 1896. A fine and imposing architectural landmark complete with clock tower, it was built for the district as a reward for becoming part of the city of Birmingham in 1891.

The library interior, 1910. Silence prevailed, with separate tables for 'Ladies' and 'Boys', while assistants fetched books on request.

The library interior, 1910.

Two views of the bright and welcoming library interior, 2000.

Moseley and Balsall Heath Institute, originally founded in 1876. The magnificent Institute building on Moseley Road, constructed by local builder John Bowen, was opened in 1883.

A programme for a dancing display at the Insitute, 1928.

The elegant entrance to the Institute.

Moseley Road Methodist Church Boys' Brigade Company, 1970.

St Patrick's Scout Group, Highgate, 1914–15.

A music workshop at St Paul's Venture Playscheme, Malvern Street, 2000.

Calthorpe Park Playcentre, 2000.

7

Public Houses

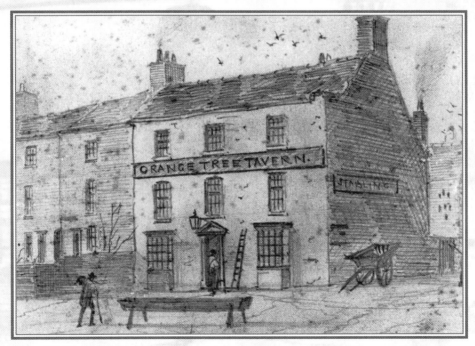

The Orange Tree Tavern on Moseley Road, near Highgate Square, 1860.

The Belgrave, on the corner of Moseley Road and Belgrave Road, 1967. This was built by William Charley, a local builder, brickmaker and entrepreneur, in 1878.

The Electric Tavern, Belgrave Road, 1961.

The Wallace, Longmore Street, on the corner of Balsall Heath Road.

The Eagle, Belgrave Road, on the corner of Longmore Street, 1962.

The Sir Charles Napier, Gooch Street, on the corner of Bissell Street. Ephraim Phillips' factory is just visible to the left.

The Hen & Chickens, Moseley Street, 2001.

The Ceol Castle, formerly the Castle and Falcon, Moseley Road, 2002.

The Waggon & Horses, on the corner of Moseley Road and Balsall Heath Road. This was one of the oldest public houses in the area, built in about 1835, but has now sadly been demolished.

The Peacock, on the corner of Darwin Street and Dymoke Street, during renovation in 1961.

The Peacock, 2000. This is now a Gibbs Mew house. No repair was made to the clock, which shows the same time in both photographs.

The Emily Arms, on the corner of Dymoke Street and Emily Street, 1961.

The Hideout (formerly the Emily Arms), 2000.

The New Inn, Moseley Road, on the corner of Edward Road. This is a fine example of Victorian pub architecture, with decorative tiling, carved woodwork and engraved glass.

The Malt Shovel in Brighton Road.

The Victoria, Runcorn Road, 2000.

The Railway, Clifton Road, on the corner of Malvern Street just beyond the railway bridge, 2000.

The Clifton, on the corner of Clifton Road and Ladypool Road, 2002.

An old postcard view of Brighton Road, showing the Brighton Hotel. This was erected in 1875 to cater for travellers using the newly opened railway station further up Brighton Road. It was another of William Charley's enterprises, and he lived here with his family for a time.

The Brighton Hotel, on the corner of Brighton Road and Ladypool Road, 2002.

The Red Lion, Ladypool Road, on the corner of Brunswick Road.

The Red Lion, 2000.

The Cannon Hill,
Edward Road, on the
corner of Court Road,
1990. It is now the
Cannon Hill Training
and Education
Centre, run by South
Birmingham College.

The Eagle, Mary
Street, 2000.

The New Moseley Arms, on the corner of Edward Road and Tindal Street.

The Old Moseley Arms, Tindal Street, 2000.

The Crown, on the corner of Hertford Street and St Paul's Road.

8

Shops & Shopping

Mrs Jones serving apples at the Jones'
greengrocery on the corner of Ladypool Road
and Colville Road.

Pinnicks, 'The Complete Home Furnishers', on the corner of Longmore Street and Balsall Heath Road, 1957. The Luxor Cinema can be seen in the background.

Wrensons Corner, Longmore Street and Belgrave Road, one of a number of food shops in the area at one time, and now gone. This picture dates from 1965.

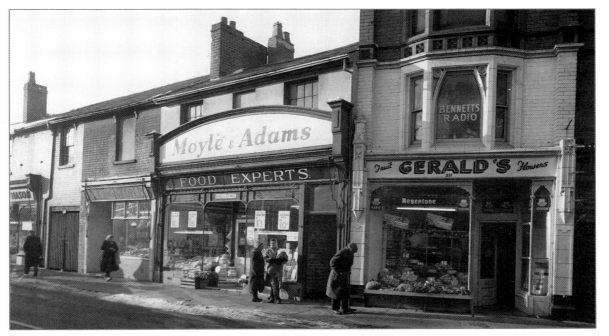

Moyle & Adams' grocers, Kingston's butchers and Gerald's Flowers on the bend in Gooch Street, 1963.

Birmingham Co-operative Society Branch No. 66, Balsall Heath Road, 1950s. Grocers, butchers and dry cleaners were all under one roof.

Gooch Street, 1955. Woolworths adjoins the Triangle Cinema on the corner of Conybere Street.

The same Gooch Street/Conybere Street site, 2000.

Local shops on the corner of Edward Road and Court Road, looking towards Calthorpe Park.

The shops seen above refurbished, and converted into the Islamic Resource Centre, 2000.

A view of Edward Road looking towards Moseley Road, 1957. The Co-op branch below is on the left-hand side; Bath Walk is on the right.

Birmingham Co-operative Society Branch No. 22 (grocers and butchers), Edward Road, 1950s.

The corner of Mary Street and Edward Road, late 1940s/early 1950s. The corner shop is Richards the chemist. The passing trams are on the City–Alcester Lanes End route.

The same corner with some of the shops now replaced by sheltered housing, 2000.

An old postcard view of the Brighton Road post office on the Moseley Road/Cromer Road corner, *c.* 1910.

The same view, 2000. The post office remains, now joined to the new Lidl supermarket.

E.J. White's China Depot, Moseley Road, on the corner of Homer Road. E.J. White's China Depot, Moseley Road, on the corner of Homer Road. This image is taken from a Bazaar Programme for Ombersley Road New Connexion Methodist Church, 1899.

The same site in 2000, now Saifee Hardware.

Birmingham Co-operative Society Branch No. 41, Ladypool Road, on the corner of Studley Street, 1950s.

The same row of refurbished shops, Ladypool Road, 2000.

The newly acquired additional premises for Shovelbottoms, motor cycle dealers, on the corner of Ladypool Road and Taunton Road, mid-1940s, There is a display of Birmingham-manufactured BSA motor cycles with sidecars.

The corner of Ladypool Road and Taunton Road, 2000.

The parade of shops at the bottom of Church Road, looking down towards Ladypool Road, 1950s.

George Mason's shop in Ladypool Road, *c.* 1901.

Taylor & Co.'s corner shop, Taunton Road and Roshven Road. Taylor's sold records and pathephones, a type of gramophone, *c.* 1920.

A complete change of business by 2000.

J. Hill, chemist and druggist, and Ladypool Road post office, on the corner of Church Road and Newport Road, *c*. 1910.

Church Road, Moseley: in 2000 the post office and chemist still remain.

Mr Stiles' pork butcher's shop in Ladypool Road, on the corner of Colville Road, 1914. The smashed windows were the result of Mr Stiles' remarks supporting Germany during the First World War while under the influence. He was forced to give up the business.

In 2000 the shop is now the Lahore Kebab House.

Frank Trippas & Son, bakers and confectioners, Ladypool Road, *c.* 1990.

The same shop is now the Lahore Asian Sweet Corner, 2002.

A typical corner shop on the corner of Woodfield Road and Ombersley Road, *c.* 1925.

Shop and its staff on the corner of Runcorn Road.

A view of Moseley Road and the corner of Belgrave Road, *c.* 1910.

S.J. Dixon & Son, painting and decorating supplier, 2002. This is a new retail development on Moseley Road.

9

Events & Celebrations

Prince Charles visiting St Paul's Venture, Malvern Street, 2001.

A St Alban's Church ceremonial procession in Conybere Street, 1913.

St Paul's Church, just before demolition, 1980. This photograph shows the congregation leaving the old church and processing to the new Church Centre in Edward Road.

Celebration time at the dedication of the new Church Centre in Edward Road, home to both St Paul's Church and the Church of Christ.

Birmingham Centenary Pageant, 1938. A young Mr Bradbury of local metalworkers Bradbury's inspects the armour made by the family firm in Highgate.

The Maypole at Highgate Road, 1902: coronation celebrations for Edward VII.

Decorations for the coronation in 1902 in Conybere Street.

Coronation Day in Beechfield Road, 1953.

Empire Day at Clifton Junior School, 1924.

Sherbourne Road School, May Festival, 1924.

Mary Street Junior School (now Heath Mount). This display dates from 1937.

A First World War peace party in Ladypool Avenue, 1918.

Jakeman Road street party for VE or VJ Day, 1945.

Balsall Heath Fun Run starting from the Sports Centre, 1991. This was part of the carnival celebrations.

The Balsall Heath Carnival, 1991: an annual and popular event.

Archbishop Desmond Tutu visiting Nelson Mandela School, 1987.

Nelson Mandela visiting the school named in his honour, October 1993.

A knobbly knees competition in Brunswick Road.

A group of children and young people at Malvern Street Playcentre (now St Paul's Venture) with their home-made go-cart, and Es Rosen, the sports worker, in 1980. Again, this is part of the carnival festivities.

10

The Second World War & Regeneration

Harbury Road Civil Defence Air Raid Wardens, 'E' Division, *c.* 1943.

Bomb damage to the premises of Parker T. Osborne, on the corner of Clevedon Road and Jakeman Walk, 1941.

Samuel Heath & Sons' factory, Leopold Street, 1941, showing bomb damage.

Rescue services in attendance at damaged property in Balsall Heath Road, 1941.

Balsall Heath Road, 2002.

Bomb damage in Gooch Street near the bridge over the River Rea in Highgate, *c.* 1942.

The same site, 2003.

Premises on Moseley Road, which was nicknamed 'Bomb Alley', opposite St Paul's Church, November 1940.

The same site today, 2002.

Runcorn Road looking from Moseley
Road, with Brighton Road railway
station buildings and platform in the
background, February 1942.

The same site, 2002.

Mary Street School after a bombing raid, early 1940s.

Ombersley Road after a bombing raid, February 1941.

Highgate Road: the results of bombing in 1940.

Highgate Road, 2002.

BALSALL HEATH LOCAL HISTORY SOCIETY

Balsall Heath Local History Society was founded in 1979 to promote an interest, understanding and appreciation of local history in Balsall Heath, Highgate and Birmingham. We warmly welcome visitors and new members to our meetings which are held on the last Thursday of the month at 7.30 p.m. at Balsall Heath Library, Moseley Road (adjacent to the swimming baths and on the no. 50 bus route). Our other publications are listed below.

Balsall Heath, A History by Valerie Hart
The development of Balsall Heath from the sparsely populated farmland and heath of the eighteenth century to the 'genteel neighbourhood' of the 1840s, the 'populous quarter' of 1891, to the busy and crowded suburb of the 1930s and 1940s. A story of change spanning two centuries.
128pp. £7.95 plus £1.00 p&p.

The Flicks
Memories of the old days at the cinema in Balsall Heath. The magic of the silver screen, from the early days of silent films to the glamour of the 1950s, is recaptured through contemporary accounts and people's memories.
48pp. £3.50 inc. p&p.

Brown Paper and Goose Grease: A Dictionary of Traditional Remedies compiled by Balsall Heath History Society
The old remedies in this book have chiefly been collected from the memories of people in Birmingham. The efficacy of the remedies is not guaranteed and in some cases they are no longer recommended!
48pp. £1.50 inc. p&p.

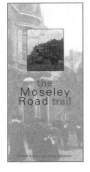

The Moseley Road Trail: The Development of the Moseley Road from the 1740s
12pp. 50p inc. p&p.

For further information telephone 0121 464 1888 or visit our website at
www.balsallheathhistory.co.uk

ACKNOWLEDGEMENTS

The Balsall Heath History Society is indebted to the many people who have donated and permitted the use of photographs, shared personal memories and passed on information without which neither this book nor the Society's archives would be possible. Many of the images contained within this publication have been obtained from old scrapbooks, albums, programmes, postcards, etc. We also wish to thank:

Richard Albutt and the Local Studies Dept of Birmingham Central Library.

The Midlands Co-operative Society Ltd (Central Region) for the supply and permission to reproduce the photographs of Co-op branches which appear on pages 93, 96 and 100.

All those who have contributed to the content of the book, including: Ian Edwards, Jacqueline Ure, Mick Turner, Pat and Albert Johnson, Nell Wilkins, Bernard Jackson, Bron and Peter Salway, Josh and Gabriel Hart, and Ann Hemming.

Many of the modern photographs were taken as part of the Society's Millennium Photographic Project, funded by the Community Fund.